French Chic

The Lady's Guide to French Style and Elegance Secrets

by Carrie Miller

Table of Contents

Disclaimer

Introduction

French chic is all about maintaining a poised, easy, appearance; always put together and never sloppy casual. Women around the world are clamoring to learn what the secret is; everyone wants a French chic style but not many know what that style actually is. Fashion editors, photographers, and fashion journalists are doing their best to explain what it is to be French chic.

The French Rivera is full of people enjoying the elegant, relaxed, atmosphere. French women stand out against this classic chic backdrop without much effort; at least it seems their style is effortless.

Compared to New York street style, French street style appears lean and just about perfect; leaving New York street style looking over done or worse, messy and unkempt.

Putting a fashion finger on the pulse of French chic is difficult. There is no telltale "fad" items drawing attention, but there is something capturing the eye. Hairstyles don't look stiff or untamed, from head to toe, French fashion is seductively simple and feminine.

Photographer Garance Dore' uses three words to sum up French chic, "Elegance is refusal". This is a very artistic, poetic, explanation but the question still lingers on the lips of would be fashionistas who are wondering what is being refused?

It seems that is the crux, and Garance Dore' packaged the explanation in a chic observation; maybe conformation is being refused.

If you want a French chic style you may need to give up a few of you long held fashion beliefs. You can't wake up one morning, throw on a French chic outfit and head off to work; French chic is more than the clothing.

Buying new clothes, accessories, or shoes, won't give you that French "it" look, and fussing with your hair will only leave you with a new hair style.

Going to France for a vacation is a wonderful choice. Freaking out and searching for the perfect "French" outfits to wear while you are there will only make you look…freaked out. Spending too much money on French fashion labels won't provide you with French style either; but it will put a whammy on your available cash.

So maybe French chic has to do with the makeup those French girls are wearing. Maybe if you purchase some French cosmetics you will bask in a bit of that French flair; nope, you will look as you always do but you will be wearing French cosmetics. There must be some way to achieve the perfect balance, the beguiling presence of French feminine…awesomeness.

Although French chic does not come in a cosmetic package, or rub off the French designer labels, there are ways to become French chic. It is all about you, and your personal charisma…or is it personal allure?

Regardless of how you word it, you must become a beguiling presence of French feminine awesomeness; you can't buy it and wear it like a perfume…if you still want to be French chic, read on.

Chapter 1 – In the Beginning-A Brief History of French Fashion

Way back, before hemlines revealed the sexy female ankle, a young French man dared to dream up a shocking, risque' smock, frock...whatever you want to call it. He gathered scraps of silk from the cutting room floor and made a dress for his sister's doll.

It was a scandalous dress, it did not require a corset, and if the doll had lungs, she would have breathed a sigh of relief! The young man was Paul Poiret, and his daring doll dress led to a century and some say longer than that, of French rule over the fashion industry.

Paul Poiret was apprenticed to an umbrella maker and it was here that he gained access to the scraps of silk. The amazing changes that followed are nothing "short" of breath taking! Hemlines went up, corsets came off and women never looked back.

They could breathe and they could partake of life's simple pleasures like sitting comfortably and feeling a warm spring breeze on their calf's. This is where the real story of French chic begins, and till this day the story is still being written.

In 1903, Poiret introduced the world of fashion to his artistic vision, and that vision was so completely awesome that he started his own house of couture. His designs were flowing and free, draping the female body, following the natural curves rather than creating them.

 Velvets and sumptuous fabrics premiered as harem pants and sultana skirts, women were dazzled and they eagerly sought his artistic fashions.

As women reveled the night away in an oxygen induced swoon, the natural lines of art nouveau were detected in the graceful flow of his liberating fashions.

A Zouave' dress designed by Pioret shows how his artistic vision expressed an art nouveau penchant for natural perfection. The dress is nothing short of an art nouveau masterpiece.

When Paul Poiret rid the fashion world of corsets, he impacted the world of fashion in a way few have repeated.

He was apprenticed to the umbrella maker because his parents believed he was too arrogant; that arrogance gave him the drive to ignore the barriers people threw in his way and focus only on his love of fashion.

He did not care what others were designing or what others thought of his designs, he cared only about being true to himself and his artistic soul.

As the fashion world changed and embraced Poiret and his designs, Coco Chanel came on the scene. Her idea of fashion was not as artistic as Poiret's, her first foray into fashion was a shop where she sold hats.

Her real entrance into the fashion world came in 1925 when she introduced her now legendary suit. The colarless jacket and close fitting skirt turned a men's fashion into an elegant female statement. The little black dress followed the suit and people couldn't get enough.

Chanel's contribution to French fashion is huge, she and Pioret are at the center of all things French chic. Her fashions were considered luxurious and elegant and she expressed her unique vision in a subtle way. She was quoted as saying, "luxury is not luxury unless it is comfortable". Are you beginning to see a theme developing?

 Hubert de Givenchi is known for his haute couture, tailored separates, elegant evening gowns, and Christian Dior is known for his refusal to accept conventional war time restrictions, and the re-introduction of feminine elegance and luxury. Comfort, freedom, personal drive, confidence...

The list of influential French fashion designers is a long one, but there is a theme that carries through from Pioret to the designers of today; confidence, freedom, and elegance emerge over and over in the art of French fashion.

 This theme is purely French and French women breathe these things in like fresh air; it is intrinsically who they are.

Chapter 2 – French Chic Fashion and You

French chic fashion is not a particular style of clothing, hairstyle, or makeup; it is hard to define. It seems that as soon as you think you have a solid definition, a French woman shows up in an outfit that doesn't seem to fit your definition.

Actually, the inability to define French chic is why French fashion is chic.

Ok, no more tongue twisters; fashion editors, photographers, and others who live and work in the fashion world have given a boat load of explanations. They are all right…French chic is a construct meant to define what it means to be a French woman.

These quotes from French fashion Icons express what it is to be French chic:

- "Before you leave the house, look in the mirror and remove one accessory" – Coco Chanel

- "Fashions fade, style is eternal" – Yves Saint Laurent

- "The dress must follow the body of a woman, not the body following the shape of the dress." – Hubert de Givenchy

Even French women explain French chic in different ways but there is a theme, regardless of the countless explanations. Here are some chic tips from French women on what to wear, how to wear it, and when to wear it.

Cécile is a French woman who is a personal shopper. She believes that chic is in the details.

- When you purchase a new pair of shoes, always remove any label or stickers on the bottom of the sole

- Scarves are a wonderful accessory that can even be worn with a white t-shirt, just make sure to always remove any tags or labels

- Sock are important too, jeans that are short enough to show your socks look great with patterned socks

- Opt for hair accessories with a bit of style instead of a regular plain hair clip, chose one with a flower, beads, or even rhinestones

The most common explanation of French chic is, "keep it simple". Keeping it simple can mean different things to different people. Keeping it simple means don't over think your style, wear what fits you best and don't overdo it with accessories.

Neutral colors are simple to wear and easy to coordinate but that doesn't mean no color; it simply means neutral will always look good.

Wearing a sequined top with a pair of patterned leggings and an arm full of bracelets is too much at once. Sequins are not for everyday wear; you won't see women walking in the streets of Paris wearing sequins to go to the book store. Patterned leggings look good by themselves; if you wear printed leggings, choose a solid, neutral color top that matches the main color in the pattern.

Bold colors, neutrals, prints, and patterns all have their place in a wardrobe, where and when you wear them is the key to French chic. Never overdo it, if you are going for French chic, less is more. One print item is more than enough for any outfit. One statement item is all you need to add a bit chic to your outfit. A unique handbag can turn a boring outfit into a chic outfit.

Wardrobe Makeover

You need to develop your own sense of style and this style should make you feel attractive and fit you and your body shape. The wardrobe you already own has the potential to be "French chic", before you run out and purchase a new wardrobe, take a look at what you own. Your style is in there somewhere.

Separate the prints from the solid colors so you can take stock of what you have. Get rid of any clothing items that do not fit you perfectly and toss out any faded items.

Put your workout clothing together and out of the way; track suits, sweat pants, track shoes, and any other items you wear to the gym need to be removed from your everyday wardrobe.

Now you should have some clothing that you love and that fits you great. This is how you transform your style from fad to chic. Now that you can clearly see what you have, you decide what you need. You may not need to purchase a thing!

When you pair your items for an outfit, make sure you pay attention to the details. Spend time creating outfits, remember, your shoes, your socks, your hair accessories, other accessories, and even your handbag need to be included in your outfit.

French chic is all about the total package and how you feel in it.

Unless you use an unobtrusive black handbag, you will need to change your pocketbook to compliment your outfit. You can add a bit of flair buy using a pocketbook with a unique shape or material. The point is, include your handbag when choosing your outfit.

Now you can simply do a search for French chic fashion and use the inspiration to create outfits from what you own. You don't need to match the brand, or the exact cut of an outfit, all you need to do is pay attention to the overall look.

View the entire look, don't focus on one item or two items; every single thing you put on is important to your style, and everything you leave out is twice as important.

Never wear something because you saw it in a fashion magazine, wear it because the cut fits you perfectly and you look and feel good in it. If you like statement pieces, only choose one, never load yourself up with chunky necklaces, patterned blouses and a loud purse.

Keep it simple, one statement per outfit; or preferably, one interesting item per outfit.

French chic is not as confusing as it seems, it is about letting your personality and style take center stage and fashion will be the result. Let neutral colors enhance your beauty not cover it up.

An awesome jacket with interesting detail can turn a bland outfit into a chic masterpiece, as long as you don't overpower it.

Chapter 3 – Chic Hairstyles

When it comes to hair, French women seem to have effortless control over their tresses. You will never have a chic look if you cut, dye, and style your hair to match the latest fashion trends. You must look good in the style you choose and you must maintain it.

When your hair cut grows out and begins to look shabby, get it cut. If your gray hairs are showing up you can choose to dye it, or work with your new color, and find a hairstyle that compliments your graying mane. Your hair cannot be too long, too short, too flat, or too curly if you choose a style and stick with it.

Chic hairstyles do not take hours to style, they are a natural match for your texture, face shape, and lifestyle. The hairstyle is not really the focus of chic; the focus is you.

You want to be comfortable in your hair and attain a look that doesn't look like it took forever to create; the key is simplicity.

A simple hairstyles looks good all the time. Bad hair days become history when your hairstyle is natural and compliments your face. Natural means you do not have to use lots of hair products to style your hair.

There are many ways to get a natural look. A good stylist will be able to help you find your perfect natural style.

Your hair should look good without lots of hair spray. If the cut compliments your facial features, it will look good right out of bed. Its true, if you have curly hair and are always straightening it, it may look good when you style it, but awful if you just let it be.

The point is, if you have naturally curly hair, work with the curls. There are hairstyles that will make your curly mane look awesome without all of the hair straightening. If you have straight hair, hairstyles with layers will give you natural volume. Work with what nature has given you and you will look chic.

When you choose to dye your hair, go with natural colors. Funky colors are great for a night at a rave, but they are never French chic. Look for a shade close to what is natural for you.

Add highlights to brighten or low lights to add depth, but make sure the color is a natural shade; no blue-black or magenta!

If you have long hair and put it up, use hair accessories that add a bit of charm to your tie back. No giant puffy scrunchies wrapped around your wrists or tied in your hair. Go for a large sleek barrette to hold back your hair.

Fad hairstyles can date you and your look. Chic never goes out of style, chic is never a fad. No rows of braids or teased bangs; look for a style that works with nothing but a blowout. It is worth your time and effort to find a fabulous hair stylist and stay with him or her.

When you are searching for a top notch stylist, recommendations from those who have a great hairstyle are worth checking out. A great stylist will be able to help you choose the right style for your hair, lifestyle, and texture.

They will be knowledgeable about different styles and who they are right for. Find yourself a stylist, they will help you attain chic, and help you maintain it.

French women prefer shiny, textured hair. Natural air dried styles are the ones sought after, but if you need a blow dry, wait a day to style it. The second day hair has more texture and some natural oil, this is the time to style. Go for a look that doesn't require much fussing.

French hairstyles are never stiff or tacky, they are flowing and healthy looking. If you put more effort into caring for your hair, the style will evolve itself.

 Healthy shiny hair is the look that goes best with a French chic style. When your hair is shiny and healthy, the length won't matter.

Chapter 4 – French Chic Makeup Tips

French chic makeup tips will help you gain an effortless beauty. Never too much and always just enough, the right makeup routine will make a world of difference in how you look and feel.

Trends in makeup come and go, but looking beautiful never goes out of style. You are aiming for beautiful and chic, a simple natural look that doesn't take forever to create.

Your makeup palette should complement your skin tone. You want to give yourself a slight blush, natural looking eyebrows and eye lashes, eyeliner that accentuates but does not over power, and no bright lipstick. These tips will provide the information you need to give yourself a French chic makeover.

Foundation and Powder

- Contouring should be subtle, as close to a natural look as you can get

- Foundation should match your complexion, if you can see the foundation, you are wearing too much

- Powder is for giving a matte finish and dealing with oily patches, it is not for covering imperfections, keep it to a minimum

- Concealer is only for small imperfection, keep this to a minimum

- Your foundation, contouring makeup, powder, and concealer should never look cakey or dried out

Eyes and Brows

- No wild colors or heavy eyeliner

- Brows should look natural not heavy, waxy, or dark

- Eye liner should accentuate your eyes without being dark and heavy

- If you can go without eyeshadow, wonderful! If not, chose a soft, earthy, palette

Cheeks and Lips

- Cheeks should have a slight blush, use a shade that matches your skin tone and go very lightly and blend

- French girls usually use two options when it comes to their lips, red, or nothing but lip balm

French women pay more attention to cleansing and caring for their skin, and less attention to applying huge amounts of makeup. Find a good moisturizer and cleanser; this will make your skin look better with less makeup.

To the French, makeup is used to accentuate, not to cover up or change. Natural beauty is what they prize and if you want a French chic look, wipe off all the makeup and start fresh.

Stay out of the sun and wear sunblock at all times. Once damage is done to the skin, it cannot be undone. Care for your skin so it will be one of your best features. The better you look without makeup, the more beautiful you are.

When your skin is healthy it shows. Your pores are more refined, and the texture is smooth and supple. Don't skimp on your skin care regime, it will improve your look better than any makeup can.

When you are shopping for makeup, do it at a store that has a makeup artist on staff. They will be able to help you find the perfect shade of foundation and a line of cosmetics and colors that will bring out your beauty in a natural way. It is worth the extra cash, and you will be shocked at great you look.

Chapter 5 – The Guide to Feminine Elegance

Elegance is not comprised of one action, thought, fashion statement, it is a way of living, of being. An elegant woman can wear a pair of jeans and a t-shirt, or a beautiful evening gown without skipping a beat. She is at home everywhere, and is never flustered; if she is, you would never know!

Your manners, your personal style, your interests and hobbies, everything that makes you individual and unique adds to your elegance.

It is all about being comfortable in your own skin, happy with your life, and in touch with yourself. You are elegant, you just need to let it show.

If you are not comfortable in an evening gown, don't wear it. If you don't like the way you look in jeans, don't buy them. Don't let fashion dictate what you wear, wear what makes you feel pretty, it's the only way you will begin to express your elegant side.

When a women can kick of her sneakers and put on a pair of heels and still look comfortable, she is elegant. The jewelry you wear is not elegant, the way you wear it is elegant...ok, so you got the picture, but how do you achieve that confidence?

You start small, make choice that make you happy, regardless of what other may think. Work at being comfortable with your decisions and don't second guess yourself. Don't ask others what they think about you or your choices, no matter how bad you may want to. Learn to rely on yourself and only yourself, it will make a dramatic difference you how you feel and how you act. You will become elegant.

Learning to accept your shortcomings can be difficult, it can make you feel inadequate. The only way you can get rid of those feelings of inadequacy is to face your shortcomings and work at lessening their impact on you and your psyche.

Everyone has personality traits they are unhappy with, most people don't love everything about themselves; but no matter what, you should always be gentle with yourself, don't judge.

Elegance is confidence in who you are. It doesn't matter what you think or feel right now, with practice you will learn to lessen negative thoughts and support positive ones. Eventually your confidence will soar; believe it or not, you impact your own confidence more than others do.

The thoughts and judgments of others can leave you with a sour taste in your mouth. The only way to gain confidence is to get rid of those feelings and learn to ignore the judgments of others.

Work at growing your confidence and it will respond, an elegant lady is waiting to take the reins, you just need to give her permission.

Self-reflection is one way to foster confidence. When you feel uncomfortable with a situation, face it, ask yourself why you feel the way you do, then make changes that will eliminate the situation.

If you are in a bad relationship and you admit to yourself that it is truly over, move on. If you can't just move on, pull away slowly, but don't sit and let it go on, that will only invite more negativity.

Always move forward in life. Don't let your past dictate your future. The past is gone, over, history, the only thing that matters now is this moment, and your future. If you always move forward you won't have time to wallow in the past.

Building confidence is all about moving through life with your eyes wide open with a receptive mind and compassionate heart. If you make a decision that makes you feel weak or out of control, forgive yourself and get on with it.

 Don't mull over the details until your eyes cross, it's over, move on and make a better choice next time.

When you are confident in yourself, you move though life with grace because you are never caught up in another time, or another place; you are always in the here and now. These tips will help you foster confidence and elegance:

- Think about what matters most to you and make an effort to achieve it

- Don't let your insecurities win, when you feel insecure, face it and make a change

- Live life according your moral code

- Don't let past mistakes instill fear of new ones

- Let the past be, live in the here and now

- Give attention to your positive achievements

- Pursue a passion

These tips are only a few ways to gain confidence in yourself and learn to express your inner elegance. When you live life according to your own morals and inclinations, you are elegant because elegance is not about what you have it is about who you are.

When things don't go as planned, learn to relax. You cannot fix things if you are in riot mode. Take things one at a time and ignore the negative thoughts and emotions. The important thing is that you are dealing with the issue in a positive, constructive way.

Sure, that sound great but remaining calm, cool, and collected while your plans end up down the drain can really wreak havoc on your day.

The truth is, the havoc already happened, there is no going back, but you do have control over how you deal with it, and that can make you feel a lot better.

The more you do this, the more confident you will become in your own ability to deal with obstacles.

So how does all this equate to French chic and elegance? The common ground for both a chic style and elegance is confidence, true confidence, not a fake, put on confidence.

When you are truly confident, your fashion is chic and your style is elegant.

When you are shopping and you see an item that you know would look wonderful on you but you put it back on the rack because you don't think you will look good in it, you need confidence.

That outfit might look fabulous on you but you will never know because you never tried it on. The point is, try it on, check it out, face your fears, get out there and life the way you want to...and you can start by trying on that outfit.

Some women can wear a frumpy sweater and look cute, another can wear that same sweater and look, frumpy.

The cute one is always cute, her personality, the way she deals with co-workers, the interesting things she talks about; these things help her look cute in that sweater.

Elegance is a state of mind, a way of being, and a love of life. To be elegant you must be confident. A confident woman can wear a red dress to the opera, she doesn't mind being stared at, in fact, she enjoys it. Her confidence allows her to be elegant.

5 Tips on How to be Elegant

- Never follow trends blindly, do what makes you happy

- Recognize and accept your feminine nature

- Never rush

- Learn to recognize simplicity and embrace it

- Never focus on yourself in a conversation, focus on others

These five tips will not increase your confidence or endow you with elegance immediately, but they will support your efforts as you work toward it. Life is what you make it, always work to make it peaceful, kind, and happy. When you do what makes you happy, you become happy.

Conclusion

Now you have some background on what it is to be French chic and elegant. Most of all you know that confidence and self-love is about all you need to achieve both elegance and a chic appearance.

So many are trying to unravel the mysteries of what it means to be French chic but no one can deliver it on a silver platter, ready to devour.

Most of the hype is just sensationalism trying to keep people entertained, the truth is, French chic is not a difficult thing to achieve or maintain.

Now that you know what it is, you can just make a few adjustments to your regular thought process and begin treating yourself a little better…the chic part follows.

Although the word chic sounds snobby or stuck up, the truth is, chic is just another word for unique. You are unique and if you allow your unique ideas to rise to the surface you will find your perfect style and without a doubt, that style will be chic.

When a woman wears a dress with confidence there is a noticeable elegance about her. She moves with confidence, enjoys conversation with confidence, and this confidence in her mannerisms makes her elegant.

Not everyone wants to be the center of attention, but an elegant woman doesn't mind if she is.

It is the French culture that spawned this all-consuming interest in French chic style. French women are just comfortable in the skin they are in…or at least they seem to be. Anyone can find the exact outfit, the right shoes, the perfect accessories, and chic may still allude them. Remember, don't be a slave to fashion, French chic involves personal style and elegance as well as an awesome outfit.

www.ingramcontent.com/pod-product-compliance
Lightning Source LLC
Chambersburg PA
CBHW070244290526
45789CB00004B/1764